A Wake for Josephine

by
Kenneth Robbins

A Wake for Josephine

Josephine

by Kenneth Robbins

A Wake for Josephine

By Kenneth Robbins

First Edition

Content Copyright © 2023 by Kenneth Robbins

Author: Kenneth Robbins
Editor: Paul Gilliland
Formatting: Southern Arizona Press
Cover Art: Karen Foster – All Rights Reserved

Published by Southern Arizona Press
Sierra Vista, Arizona 85635
www.SouthernArizonaPress.com

ISBN: 978-1-960038-19-7

Poetry

"Oh, Jake," Brett said, "we could have had such a damned good time together."

. . .

"Yes," I said. "Isn't it pretty to think so?"

The Sun Also Rises
Ernest Hemingway

Special thanks to:

My wife, Dorothy Dodge Robbins, my fellow writers Genaro Ky Ly Smith, April Honaker, Caleb Elkins, and Jon Stewart.

A very special thanks to Karen Foster for her remarkable art work and to Paul Gilliland for his editorial expertise.

Contents

Kenneth Robbins

Cast of Characters

Josephine Tapper-Screed, early twenties, not pretty but
 cute, petite, unsure
   Adjunct instructor of English at the University, a new hire
   When she smiles, she ignites her entire face
   When she cries, her whole body weeps
   When she speaks, few listen
   When she leaves, few notice

Blayne Crumbley, late twenties, handsome in a rugged way
   Dreams of being a professional golfer
   Prone to sneering
   Rarely laughs except at his own jokes
   Walks with a swagger
   Proud of his groin

Lee Screed, mid-thirties, balding, growing a gut
   His dreams swallowed by the demands of responsibility
   Labors over numbers
   Despondent upon being deserted
   Treats others harshly as he was harshly treated

Josephine's Parents, inheritors of a Southern culture
   She, patient, caring, tied to the home
   He, former farmer turned insurance salesman
   She, deeply religious, loves her only child
   He, unpredictable, trusts no one

Others and there are many.

Kenneth Robbins

Josephine and Lee, Married,
(A Duologue)

Scene 1

HIM--Vegetable beef soup?
HER--Um hm.
HIM--We had tomato soup with cheese last night.
HER--Uh yeah.
HIM--Can't you cook anything that doesn't come in a can?
HER--Not really.
HIM--I guess we could eat out more.
HER--I don't like McDonald's.
HIM--There are other restaurants.
HER--I don't like Burger King, either.
HIM--Then I'll order a pizza.
HER--And waste the veggie beef soup?
HIM--Boomer'll eat it. He'll eat anything.
HER--I hate that dog. He'll throw up again.

Scene 2

HIM--There's thirty-five dollars not accounted for.
HER--Hm?
HIM—Thirty-five dollars missing.
HER--I needed shampoo.
HIM—Thirty-five dollars for a bottle of shampoo?
HER--I require the gentle touch.
HIM--My shampoo only costs three ninety-eight.
HER--I can tell.
HIM--What do you mean?
HER--Now I know why your hair's falling out.
HIM--We can't afford thirty-five-dollar shampoo.

HER--I'm working now. Of course we can.
HIM--You don't bring enough home to . . .
HER--I like my job.
HIM--Good. I'm glad there's some value to be had . . .
HER--I enjoy it.
HIM--Flirting with a bunch of college freshmen.
HER--Sometimes, sure, why not.

Scene 3

HER--I love you, Lee.
(Silence)
HER--I said. Love ya Lee.
(Silence)
HER--This much and this much and . . .
HIM--Will you let me sleep?
HER--Good night, grumpy pumpkin.
(Silence)
HER--Ooo. Is Mr. Pumpkinhead showing a little life?
(Silence)
HER--Knock knock, who's that at my door?
HIM--Will you shut up.
HER--Gladly.
(Silence)
(Silence)
HIM--Mmmmm.

Scene 4

HIM--Grading papers. Again?
(Nothing)
HIM--That's all you do. Grade papers.
HER--Will you leave me alone?
HIM--With pleasure.
(Door slams as he leaves.)

Scene 5

HER--Lee? When're you coming home?
(Nothing)

Scene 6

(A note)
HIM--Gone to a bar, don't ask which one.

Lee's Lament: Too Much/Too Little

Imagine this: me, ten inches long,
no hair, no teeth, ten fingers, two feet
and lungs with a siren's song.
Now that I am five feet longer,
with most teeth, ten toes, two hands
and muscles a good bit stronger:
the same human creation,
the same me, now as then.
Sans love
as of today when she said "Leave."
which I did
with an acceptance that I,
even now, cannot conceive.

I have trouble
imagining me at three feet or even four,
me with frizzled hair still
and teeth falling free,
me with few words to express
what I most despairingly need,
the thing I called "My Love."

She said get, so I go,
I don't know why though.

"Welcome home, my boy," my mom says,
though I don't know why.
"She tossed me out," I say,
and she says, "Good.
I never liked that woman from the start."
Like. Such a shapeless word,
equal to Love
in its own way.
"You brought her here," she says,
"And I knew. She had no heart.

She would do you dirt.
You my most precious one."

I gather my guts and stop by our place
and struggle to resist the urge
to smash her dainty face.
I ask, "What did I do wrong?"
And she says, "I suppose
you loved me too much."

I gather my things and leave again
thinking tomorrow we might
perhaps attempt another start.
So little do I know
the content of her heart.

Her claim: Loving too much.
To love at all is so little,
for a man like me who was
reared to be brittle. But
to love too much?
That remains an impossible riddle.

Now gone,
I know my love for her
was less than I thought.
Love too large, love too small.
Fail to love at all.
What else is there except affection
reciprocated and shared,
call it what you will.
But too much love?
What pain you wrought.
Too little more likely than not.

Blayne's Lament: Mine

All the good ones have been taken.
I've said this hundreds of times,
and meant it, mostly.
Then, she entered my life, my angel.
Josie, oh glorified Josephine.
She begins my life anew
each time we clasp our hands,
each time our lips compress,
each time my sperm explodes inside her womb.
I inform her so she knows: she is
Mine.

She is all that I need,
and need her is my all.
Need her sweetness to leaven my darkness,
her brain to balance my dullness,
her gentle touch to replace my blows,
her faith to quell my despair.
Nothing else is necessary,
as long as she is
Mine.

Mine.
Only mine.
I ask nothing more than that
she belongs to me.
Only me.
All mine.

No other claim but
Mine.
Any claim other than
Mine,
I will deal with
accordingly.

Josephine's Lament: The Sully Touch

What I touch I sully:
Taint, defile, soil, tarnish, stain, blemish, pollute, spoil, mar,
    besmirch, befoul.
In grammar school, I tainted the classroom with my
    questions.
In church, I defiled the pew on which I sat by not
    questioning enough.
In dating, I soiled the lips that I kissed.
Friendships I tarnished without fail.
My pet collie named "Fred" I stained with petting.
With cheap creams I blemished my face.
I polluted my body with diet cola.
I spoiled my hair with impatience.
I mar my life with all that I touch.
I sullied my job and am not worthy of being employed.
I sully all that I touch, all that I hold dear.

I besmirch my name
and befoul my future
and pray to a sneering God
that I might lose the gift of the Sully Touch.

I left momma's home and failed in that.
I married Lee and quickly sullied that as well.
I left Lee to explore my defiling life.
And without looking far, found this other,
a man with a touch like mine,
a man full of smiles and idiotic jokes,
a man with needs so akin to mine,
a man who is determined
to sully me.

Night Out

The bar stool is too high.
The air filled with smoke,
all second-hand.
The top of the bar sticky,
residue from previous sojourners
like Josie and me.
The old-fashioned juke-box
litters the place with
old-fashioned tunes,
mostly base and snare drums
and squeaky female vocals.

I don't like it here.

Too many people, mostly male,
with smelly armpits and
dirty fingernails, with
cigarettes hanging loose
from smirking lips
and pants smudged
with last month's grime.

Really don't like it here.

I am, though, here--
in spite of my resistance, and
at Josie's insistence,
her need to break free.
From what, I ask her, but
she doesn't seem to know.
So I sit uneasily on the hard bar stool
sipping my sour through a straw,
afraid to put my mouth on
the glass's edge, afraid
of what I might catch
and take home to my kids.

    I don't like that she brought me here.

There is this guy who keeps
hitting on us, on her more than me,
Josie being the cute one,
him and his two hangers-on,
slurrishly laughing at the tepid
sexual innuendos the first one makes.
Thinks he's funny,
thinks he's the man,
him with his barrel chest and
low-hanging dungarees and
his muddy hiking boots—
Been hunting, he says, out in the woods
when all along, what I was hunting for
was waiting for me right here,
sitting like a princess,
waiting for me to do my thing.

    I don't like men like him.

Truth be told, any man,
just don't like them.
I don't want another drink
though I get one
wanted or not.
I don't belong in a place like this,
where men with dagger eyes slice
us to bits and lick their lips
in anticipation.

       Here and me don't mix.

I might as well not be here,
that's what I tell her:
Might as well be home.
Okay, she says to me, and grins,
like she's been here before,
done this time and time again.
She says through that grin of hers
Bye, then.
See you tomorrow.

       I don't want to leave her alone
       but I do.

A hanger-on trails me
to the door and opens it for me
and follows as I find my car.
I know what you need, Miss Priss,
he says to me as I unlock the door.
What you need is what I got, he says,
and moves in for more.
The vile of mace is in my purse
easy to grasp and point as I say,
I got all I need, thank you.
It is his time to be afraid as he
considers what this wacky woman
might do with a squirt of juice.

Then, he is gone.

I breathe freely in the reservoir of my car
and wonder: What secrets might
Josie have in her purse
in case she needs to use them?
I know her.
Miss Unprepared.
Miss Trust Everybody in the World.
Miss Sitting Target If There Ever Was One.

Wish she was more like me.
Then she would think twice
before saying *adios* to Lee.

Missing at Home

Quiet hurts.
It hurts the ears.
It hurts the eyes.
It hurts all over
especially at night when
you expect the quiet.
Now it's just you.
You alone.
After seven years, only you.

The You that you are yells at the closets.
You shout down the pillows.
You bellow from your bathtub
for no reason except
it is only you.
You alone.

Quiet brings doubt.
It blurs your thinking.
It slurs your speaking.
It curbs your sleeping.
It disturbs your being.
Is there no cure
for a quiet that you made
with your failure
with your complaints
with your restraints
with all that you do?

There is a difference
between quiet and silence.
Silence is when someone is there
but making no noise.
Quiet is when you're alone with
nobody to break it apart.
So, noise free.

You've earned it.
You've made it.
You've lost a way to remove it.
So, live with it
as best you can.

Adjuncts

Monday

1: A Faculty Office: Two Voices

KID--Excuse me, ma'm?

PROF--Yes, what is it?

KID--I'm in Ms. Tapper-Screed's class, nine a.m., room 244, freshman comp.

PROF--So?

KID--She's not here.

PROF--Who?

KID--Ms. Tapper-Screed. We've been waiting over fifteen minutes.

PROF--Who?

KID--All of us, those in the class.

PROF--Did she announce no class today?

KID--No, ma'm.

PROF--Did Ms. Screed send a surrogate?

KID--We're all there, waiting.

PROF--Well, go back, wait some more.

KID--How long should we wait?

PROF--Ms. Tapper-Screed's an adjunct. Fifteen minutes? You've already waited long enough.

KID--Should I –

PROF--Go away. Tell the others to leave. And shut my door. I have papers to grade.

2: Departmental Break Room: Three Voices

1--She's not missed a class before, has she?

3--Not to my knowledge.

2--This'll get her fired if she doesn't show.

3--Maybe she doesn't care.

1--She's an adjunct. She has to care.

3--Not showing? No notice? So much for caring.

2--I can't believe it. She's not the type.

3--What type is that?

2--Sweet. Cheery. Dedicated. Completely dedicated.

3--That's apparent. Ha!

1--I heard she was having problems at home.

2--Where'd you hear that?

1--She told me. Friday, at lunch.

2--I don't think I know her. Who is she again?

1--Adjunct. First term. She graduated last spring, masters. Her first job-- this.

3--Obviously can't count on her, can we?

2--Maybe something's wrong.

1--Do you know where she lives?

2--No, don't you?

1--Well, she's already missed her class. Nothing we can do now.

3--Got papers to grade.

2--Me, too. The never-ending task, flood of shitty writing.

1--You ask me, she's smart, saying the heck with this job.

2--If you hear from her, let me know.

1--Why?

2--She's sweet. She makes me laugh. I like her.

3--I wouldn't know her if I saw her.

1--Adjuncts. Never count on adjuncts.

3--We're all adjuncts, for pity's sake.

2--And Josephine is showing us our way out.

3--Who is she again?

Wednesday

3: A Faculty Office: Two Voices

KID--Excuse me, ma'm.

PROF--You again?

KID--She's not here.

PROF--Who are you talking about?

KID--Ms. Tapper-Screed. We're waiting. Monday, she's not
here. Today . . .

PROF--Knock on her door. Her office is next to mine.

KID--Have you seen her?

PROF--No, but I've not been looking.

KID--She's not answering.

PROF--Obviously not there.

KID--What should we do?

PROF--How should I know?

KID--Aren't you a professor?

PROF--Of course, but that doesn't make me God.

KID--I like Ms. Tapper-Screed's class. She's fun.

PROF--Well, I'm sorry she's ruining your good time.

KID--Seriously, ma'm, I'm worried. Is it like her to miss
class like this?

PROF--How should I know. I hardly know the woman.

KID--She's great, really. Really great.

PROF--I'm sure.

KID--Seriously, we're worried, Professor.

PROF--Well, worry someplace else.

4: Departmental Break Room: Three Voices

1--I'm convinced something's happened.

3--What?

1--I don't know. Something.

2--You think she's been what, kidnapped?

3--On a lark, most likely.

2--Well, why not? It's been known to happen.

3--Not in Newtown.

1--Newt's just like any other town. I don't know.

2--What's it been, three days?

1--Should we talk to the chair?

3--And bother her? No way. Tapper's just an adjunct.

1--Still. . .

3--It's not your problem. Not mine, either.

2--Tapper's brought this on herself. Let her deal with it.

3--Yeah, let her deal with it. She's only an adjunct.

1--Yeah? So am I.

3--You gotta watch yourself, when you're an adjunct.

1--Gotta go. Class.

2--Lunch?

1--Sure. Give me a sec.

3--Sick of having adjunct's dissed.

2--Me, too.

3--I'll go to my grave, an adjunct. Probably.

1/2--Me, too.

5: Friday: A Hallway: One voice

PROF--Who put this camellia in Ms. Tapper-Screed's door!

Her Face

Josephine.
Her face screams at me.
To me.
Through me.
From the board,
newly installed
at the local Walmart Neighborhood Market.

The Board of the Missing.

Six rows of faces, five rows deep.
Thirty photos.
Pasted on the Walmart wall.

It is her, her face on the Board.
Third from the left, second row.
With her name, Josephine Tapper-Screed,
inscribed in black ink an inch below her open-mouth, toothy
grin.
The same grin I had studied for a year.
Two years ago.

Josie, I want to say:
Why are you on the
Walmart Board of the Missing?
I remember you the
special things that belong only to you:
Sweet,
soft-spoken,
tender with your dog,
challenged by your classes,
charming with your friends,
curt with all others.

Yet, you are here?

Your face,
pasted on the board?
Here, in this town?
So far from where you live?
Or perhaps,
once lived?

"Get outta the way, fella," the shopper hisses at me,
shoving past.
I'm in the way,
standing transfixed near the exit of the Market,
two bags in hand.
I apologize for that.

But it's Josephine to blame.
She holds me.
Me, stupefied.
Me. Confounded.
Curious.
How could *you*,
sweet Josephine,
be among "the missing?"

No Body
(A Monologue)

With no body, there is no crime.
The woman is missing, nothing more.
Gone missing, happens all the time.
Gone missing, worth looking for?

My job is to detect, if I can,
What might have led to this particular state,
A state of "gone missing," that's all,
Just one fact to finally relate

Is all I ask, one concrete relevant fact
To share with family and friends, concerned
With the woman's well-being, being well,
When "missing" is all that I have learned.

Suspects I have, but no misdeed so far,
I have no body, so there is no crime.
If no crime, then why am I involved?
A woman's gone missing, happens all the time.

Other things, I have other things to do.
Sorry folks, I'm done with this.
She'll turn up, they always do,
Turn up and laugh at us--with sardonic bliss.

Been to the beach, she'll say,
Or to the mountains, or abroad.
Her body intact, no harm at all,
Sun burnt and nothing more.

There's no body, though we've been searching,
So no crime. But this case, the missing one,
Haunts my waking and sleeping.

Why her? She won't leave me alone.

Why her. Missing is not who she is.
Being gone is not what she does.
Being in touch is who she has been.
Not this. Not. So I'm done.

Last Seen . . .
(A Monologue)

Yes, sir, I know Josie Tapper.
She and me went to junior high together.
She went on, finished at Newtown High.
Me, I dropped out.
Couldn't take the teachers
or having to read.
Hated reading then.
Still do, I guess.

Yes, sir, she was by here that Sunday.
I was on the register all day that day.
She come in, bought a diet soda.
And a pack of soda crackers.
I kidded her, said she was gonna get fat.
I deduced she was hungry or something.
That Josie could never be called fat.
Skinny as a bean pole.
But cute, though.
Nice hair.
Course, she knew that.
Went to her head some,
if you know what I mean.

Yes, sir, there was a man with her.
Sometime around two I guess.
He went to the bathroom.
Didn't speak to him.
He didn't speak to me.
He was like in a hurry,
like he was gonna bust or something.
Didn't look all that happy,
neither of them did.
She popped her diet soda

And it spewed all over her.
Made her mad.
Made me mad, too.
I mean, I'm the one who had to clean it up.

Then, he come back from the back.
Said "Get in the car, we gotta go."
Sharp, like he was put out about something.
She paid me for the things she'd bought
and apologized for making such a mess.
Then, she followed him outside to the car.
A Honda Civic, blue, sorta dirty.
Or maybe it was white.
And they drove off.
Heading that way, toward Ansley.

Yes, sir, I heard she was missing.
News travels slow around here.
But I heard it okay.
You think that fella I seen her with
kidnapped her? Or something?
He didn't seem all that happy when he was here.
But then, happiness ain't something
you can order about, now is it.
Sure we got a closed circuit TV.
We're up-to-date around here.
Only, we generally don't turn the thing on
unless we got an inkling that something's
going on.
So, no, sir, we ain't got no footage left
of that Sunday afternoon.

You got a photo of the man?
Lemme see.
Yes, sir, that's her alright.
Sweet smile.
And that's him, that's the guy

who used our washroom.
Good looking fella.
If I'm to be kidnapped,
I'd want somebody that looks like him
to do me.
Wouldn't you?

Mama's Lament for the Miracle Child

When she entered a room,
It was as if a light had turned on.
My daughter, my miracle child,
Glowed with goodness and love.

"Mama, you're my bestest friend,"
She was oftentimes heard to say,
Not only to me, but to anyone:
"Daddy, you're my onliest beau."

"Daddy, you're my building block."
"LeeLee, you're my comfort zone."
"Mama, you're my Gibraltar Rock."
"I could not live were it not for you."

She phoned me every day, literally,
Never failed, after her work was done.
Called me, greeted me with joy,
Such joy, such enormous love and need.

Once when her smile was weak, I asked
"Is that man treating you well, my dear?"
And she answered like a candle
Going out, "As well as I deserve."

"You deserve only the best,"
I should have said, but didn't.
It's her life, not mine, I erroneously felt.
"Only what's best," I should have said.

There came that day, that dreaded day
When my phone did not ring,
And I knew, here, in my core, something
Had wrested my miracle child from me.

The Car
(A Report)

We find it two blocks from the missing girl's flat.
It is locked.
It fits the description we have been given.
A Honda Civic, silver, pale blue interior.
Missing its tag.
Parked partially on the curb.
Motor cold from sitting.
Residue of rain from two nights before.

We breech the locked door.
Registration: Josephine Tapper-Screed.
Interior wiped clean.
No fingerprints.
Smudge of mud on break petal.
The last radio station on the dial is NPR.
Classical music junk.

The driver's seat is locked in the deep back position.
Deduction: the last person to drive the vehicle
is at least six feet tall, probably more.
Description of the car owner is that she, the missing,
is a petite five foot two.
Conclusion: the owner was not the last person to drive this
car.

Confirmation: from the owner's father:
"It's hers.
It's my kid's.
I helped her pick it out.
Last year.
We bought it for her last year."

We find the spare set of keys in the owner's apartment,
stowed in her computer desk drawer.

The Civic is impounded as evidence.

End of entry.

A Dream of Josie, Lost in the Woods

> *Here*
> *I am here*
>
> *I am here*

On our way home from Opulence,
with Hubert behind the wheel,
I am startled awake.
It is dusk on a dreary day.

We have been to Opulence,
attending a gathering of old men
and almost as old women
and even older music,

our annual tribute to the
masters of folklore found
in the lower quadrant
of our fair and peaceful state.

It is magical, the effect
of folklore in this part of the world.

> *Here*
> *I am here*

I am sleeping fitfully
following our two-day fest,
gladly forfeiting the guide of the car
to the capable hands of Hub.

I am startled awake
and sit forward with a jerk.
"You okay, sweet?" is Hub's concern
and I do not have an answer.

Perhaps it was the emotions
evoked by the traditional music
a residual that filtered into my dream,
or more like, it was me and nothing else at all.

"I just felt," I say, casual out of need,
"I felt something strange," not knowing
at all what it was that I meant.
It was Josie, I know, dear, missing Josie,

> *Here*
> *Over here*

"Josie's been missing two weeks now,"
I say, or think I say, or want to say.
Josie, a kid I had hired to teach
within the adjunct program, a late add-on.

"You thinking of that missing girl?"
Hub asks, knowing the answer.
"I think of little else," I say,
"Only not usually in my dreams."

"Tell me," he says, an advocate for
the solemn interpretation of dreaming.
"If you want," he adds, for he knows
how personally I have taken Josie's absence.

I gaze about me, at the pines
struggling to grow tall,
second growth in this area
we know locally as Ansley.

Thick, uncontrolled growth, mostly vines
and a natural haunt for deer
and squirrels and rabbits and

opossums that enjoy playing dead.

"In my dream," I say, unclear even to me,
as I speak. "She spoke. She said, 'Here,
I am here.'" The woods are impenetrable.
"Here, I am here." I say, still unclear.

"There," I say, gesturing to the woods,
"She has disappeared and could possibly
be there," with a broad sweep of my arm.
"There, even there." Who knew, I didn't,

Here
I am

A Wake for Josephine

The Search, Part 1

In the missing girl's apartment is a computer.
We searched it.
Thoroughly.
Mr. Crumbley's fingerprints were all over it.
The girl was reported missing
October 7, confirmed.
On that day, someone on the computer
had purposed a number of searches.
Curious items:
golf equipment
and porn sites.
More of the later than the former.
Searches were logged: October 7, eleven p.m.
Mr. Crumbley admits to being the searcher
on Ms. Tapper-Screed's equipment.
He states that he was her roommate.
Confirmed.
They had co-inhabited the flat for several months.
He is a self-proclaimed Professional Golfer.
Is there any money in that, I ask him.
Not a cent, he says.

Except: Ms. Tapper-Screed's last known action
on October 7 prior to disappearance
was writing him, Mr. Crumbley, a check on her personal
    account
in the amount of three thousand dollars.
The check, he says, was the woman's gift to him,
to help him purchase the golf equipment he needs
to support his so-called profession.
Expenditure of funds: unconfirmed.
This is confirmed: Mr. Crumbley cashed the check.
Note: what about the porn? Was that part of the deal?

Our search of the premises confirmed:

Mr. Crumbley had indeed been inhabiting the flat
as he claims. With Ms. Tapper-Screed.
He has since moved on.
Moved down south.
Said he couldn't maintain the rent by himself.
They got lots of golf courses down south.
Don't worry: we've got him in our sights.

The Gun
(A Duologue)

COP--Josie owned a gun?

POP--She owned a gun.

COP--What kinda gun?

POP--A gun that shoots.

COP--You know this for a fact?

POP--Course, she's my kid.

COP--Where'd she get a gun?

POP--I give it to her.

COP--How come?

POP--So she be safe.

COP--Safe from what?

POP--They be some mean sorts of fellas out there.

COP--All sorts, yeah.

POP--Guess you know that.

COP--So, where's this gun? Where'd she keep it?

POP--Wouldn't know.

COP--But it was a good gun, you say, shoots and all.

POP--It was a worthy pistol, I can tell you that.

COP--How do you know?

POP--I took her shooting, taught her to shoot.

COP--So, she knew how to use it?

POP--What good's a gun if you don't know how to shoot?

COP--And she had bullets?

POP--What good's a gun that ain't loaded?

COP--Well, I guess we gotta list that gun as missing, too.

POP--Hate that word, missing.

COP--Somebody musta took that gun.

POP--Why would anybody want to take her gun? It weren't
   much.

COP--If we knew that, sir, we'd know where your daughter's
   at.

POP--You saying somebody took my girl and her gun?

COP--We're saying the gun ain't here, nothing more than
    that.
POP--Why would anybody want that stupid gun? Such a
    puny thing.
COP--I thought you said it could shoot.
POP--Could and did, shoot straight.
COP--Then it can't rightly be called a stupid gun, can it.
POP--I'd do it again, mister, sure as shooting.
COP--Do what again?
POP--Give my baby a gun.
COP--I'm sure you would, sir, I'm sure you would.
POP--Gotta protect ourselves from the crazies out there.
COP--And a gun's the only thing for that, right?
POP--You got that right.

Holes

My son and I don't share much.
Talk ball scores
and who's hot on the links.
Masters is coming
so we talk of that.

In a bit, I ask,
Where's that cute little girl of yours?
I liked her a lot.
He squirms a tad,
sitting uneasy on the porch swing.
I broke that off, he tells me.
A surprise to me.
She seemed to dote on him
and him on her.
He had actually brought little Josie by
a month or so ago, proud and strutting
Like he had hit a hole in one.
And I ask,
Broke it off? How come?
He shrugs and says,
She was going back to her old man.
That no good Lee Screed, old bald-headed Lee.
How come? I ask again.
He just shrugs, like when
You triple bogey a hole
And have to go on to the next.

In another bit, he says,
He can't have her, though.
She's mine or nobody's.
I took care of that.

Took care?
What do you mean, Blayne?

She won't be going back to Lee
nor anybody else. I swear.

Something in his manner turns my head awhirl.
I know my kid, the way he thinks,
the way I tried as hard as I could
to change.
Something in him holds tight
to whatever he feels he is due,
and I don't follow him when he's like that.
Would he turn the girl loose
or cling to her tight
or do something else that I can't figure out.
What he says,
Not going back to Lee,
shivers my backbone
and I want to know more
if there is more to know.

How can you be sure of that? I ask.

There is a quiver in his voice
when he says, "I'm damn sure."
There's a sliver of snot oozing out his nose
as he adds: "That Lee's nothing but
a hole in the ground,
So I give her another hole.
One made especial for her.
She found her hole.
Let her lie in it."
He swipes the snot with his sleeve.

We eat dinner and then he leaves,
gets in that car, a silver Honda Civic
that couldn't possibly be his.
I call the State Patrol and ask
Is that college professor

from up Newtown way
still missing,
and they say she sure is.
So I tell them where they should look next,
in the woods near Ansley
and be on the lookout
for an old well or more like
a hole in the ground.

I pray that once found,
the hole is empty, nothing there.
I also pray silently
for the soul of my son.

A Wake for Josephine

The Search, Part 2

Like looking for a needle in a hayfield.
Only, not a needle.
A girl.
A woman gone missing.
Missing for some time now, they say.
Not a hayfield, either.
A thick, overgrown, vine-infested third-growth pines.

Why look here?
These woods are for hunting game,
not lost gals.

They say she's a looker.
They say she's real young.
They say she's a college teacher.

So.

What's a good looking, tender-age broad,
and a college professor to boot,
doing missing in a place like this.

Maybe she don't want to be found.
Maybe somebody don't want her to be found.

Waste of time.
A waste of everybody's time,
not just mine.

Should be home, watching the Saints.
No right-minded female would choose
a place like this to go missing in.

Waste of ever-loving time.

Could be home, watching the Saints.

Flowers for Josephine

At first, the janitors left the flowers untouched. They were doing no harm. They were fragrant, especially the roses and the camellias. But each morning of that first week of missing, the collection became a pile and the pile tended to impede movement along the hall. On the second Friday of Josephine's disappearance, the Head of the Department sent out her decree: cease with the flowers already; enough was enough.

With her direction, the janitors cleared away the fragrant hoard, placing them gingerly and with reverence into a wheeled bin. But after several trips to the lift and thence to the dumpster on the edge of the parking lot, the ginger and reverent care dissipated. Just get the job done, as quickly as possible, no time to dawdle, no desire to be late for break. Besides, the flowers left residue on the floor that required the extra task of sweeping and in a few spots, actually mopping, generating more effort than the treatise toward sympathy was worth.

The third Monday of Josephine's missing, more flowers appeared outside her office door. This time they were more abundant, some in bunches, some in vases, others in wreaths. The hallway by midweek appeared to replicate Princess Di's commemorations from several decades before. Only this one was in the way of the business of the Department, leading the Department Head to post a flat sheet that read: "No more flowers. Ms. Tapper-Screed is not dead, so no more flowers, PLEASE!"

Didn't work, the plea for normalcy. The janitors still, and with growing begrudgement, hauled the undesirable dead plants to the over-full dumpster on the edge of the parking lot. Someone with a black magic marker scrawled across the Department Head's message the words, "Come back, Ms. Screde. We mis you."

Ms. Josephine Tapper-Screed, you must recall, was an adjunct hire, and as such, due only a modicum of respect from her fellow faculty. The outpouring of care on her behalf caused the assistant, associate, and full professors a sense of jealousy, even envy: If one of them decided not to return to work, would he or she be so deeply missed?

But the bouquets and wreaths continued to appear, even beyond the third full week of the adjunct's disappearance. Many felt that the wreaths were appropriate; maybe, they felt, it was likely that Ms. Josephine Tapper-Screed would not be returning after all. It was difficult for anyone to think positive thoughts about her absence. But then, that's the nature of human nature, to imagine the worst even as one longs for the best?

Eventually, flowers in bunches ceased to appear, leaving only a single red rose stuck each morning carefully into the jamb of Josephine's office door. Each morning, a newly cut, aromatic rose. It was there when the first patrons of the hallway appeared and it remained until after the last had left for the day. No one knew who was responsible for that single lovely gesture. It made no difference who since the last rose disappeared on the afternoon of the final day of the academic term. The tribute to Josephine's memory slipped comfortably into the recesses of the hallway and did not return as a new adjunct moved into the office at the beginning of another quarter of work.

A Wake for Josephine

Found
(A Duologue)

A knock at a door.
The door opens.

COP--Sorry to bother you on a Sunday afternoon, Ms. Tapper.

MOM--You're always welcome, Sheriff.

COP--Just a deputy, ma'm, just a deputy.

MOM--Deputies, too. Always welcome.

COP--Got some news for you, ma'm, you and Mr. Tapper.

MOM--He ain't home right now. You can tell me.

COP--I could come back later, when he's home.

MOM--You came here to tell me something.

COP--I should wait.

MOM--Tell me.

    Silence

COP--Well. . . looks like we've found your daughter. Like we promised.

MOM--Oh, God. Oh, glory. Where is she? Is she okay?

COP--Maybe you best sit, Ms. Tapper. Please?

MOM--You found her, praise Jesus.

COP--I guess you could say it was something of a miracle, ma'm.

MOM--My miracle child.

COP--Finding the body where we did.

MOM--Body?

COP--Yes, ma'm. In a well. In the woods west of Ansley. A dry, deserted well.

MOM--Then, she's –

COP--Yes, ma'm. I'm so sorry.

MOM--Oh, God.

    Silence
    More silence.

COP--Can I get you something, Ms. Tapper? A glass of water?

MOM--No. You say you've found a body. But it's not Josephine. Not my Josie.

COP--It's Josie, ma'm.

MOM--No, not possible. If my daughter was dead, I'd feel it. In here.

COP--Ma'm—

MOM--Right here. You're mistaken. My Josie's not . . .

COP--I went to school with her, Ms. Tapper. We dated off and on, remember?

> *Silence.*

MOM--Where is she? I must see her.

COP--We've taken her to the morgue. In a case like this –

MOM--Case?

COP--Josie was murdered, ma'm.

MOM--Oh, Lord Jesus.

> *Silence.*

COP--You'll be able to see her after the inquest and autopsy. A couple of days more than likely.

MOM--How?

COP--Ma'm?

MOM--Murdered how?

COP--Gun shot wound. To the breast.

MOM--Oh . . Did she suffer?

COP--No. No, don't think so. The bullet severed her heart. She would have died within seconds.

MOM--Oh. I'll have to tell her father.

COP--I can tell him if you want.

MOM--This may kill him.

COP--Seriously. No problem. I can wait . . .

MOM--Me, too. Could kill me, too.

> *Silence.*
> *More silence.*

COP--I am so sorry, Ms. Tapper. She was such a kind and generous. . .

MOM--Yes. She . . .

COP--I've gotta be going, I guess. Can I do anything . . .

MOM--You found her in a well?

COP--Yes, ma'm. About twelve feet deep. Deep in the woods. Squirrel hunting land.

MOM--She was shot in a well?

COP--Well, no. She was shot and then dragged to the well and . . . dumped.

MOM--My daughter was dumped?

COP--I'm sorry. I should of said lowered into. Dumped was callous of me.

MOM--Was she covered at all?

COP--Only with leaves. A thin layer of leaves.

MOM--Somebody pointed a gun at my baby's heart, killed her, then dumped her remains in a hole in   the ground. What kind of human being would do such a thing.

COP--We don't know yet, but we'll find out.

MOM--That husband of hers. That Lee. I never trusted him.

COP--We're pretty sure that Lee had nothing to do with this. But the man she was living with—

MOM--Blayne something, I forget his name.

COP--It was Blayne Crumbley who led us to search the Ansley woods.

MOM--He's confessed?

COP--No, ma'm. He bragged. Couldn't keep his mouth shut.

MOM--Bragged.

COP--To his father. Bragged about putting his kill in a worn-out well in the Ansley woods. He didn't specify what kill he was talking about. But his daddy put two and two together and came up with what we found. Blayne's daddy was afraid he was going to be next. That's why he told us.

MOM--He seemed like such a friendly sort.

COP--We've arrested him already, ma'm. No need to worry.
        Silence.

MOM--Did he do it?

COP--All evidence that we have points to him.

MOM--Why? We had him and Josie for dinner on Labor Day.

COP--We don't know.

MOM--But *why?*

COP--We'll probably never know, ma'm.

MOM--Do you think he did it?

COP--We're positive.

> *Silence.*

MOM--May God toss his wretched soul into the fire and brimstone of everlasting Hell.

COP--I could live with that. Sure. I could live with that.

Police Department Form C-652 (Coroner's Div.)
Autopsy: Case No. 5488691

Victim's Name: Tapper-Screed, Josephine

Sex: Female   **Age:** 30   **Race:** Caucasian
Weight: 117 (approx.)   **Height:** 5'2"

Description of Corpse:

Victim's body decomposed beyond recognition, identity
determined by dental records. C: Dr. Harold Crossly, Crossly
Dental Services, Newtown. Clothing intact. No sign of struggle
beyond abrasions on back caused by being dragged from site of
execution to site of disposal. Body partially covered with loose
leaves. Assessment: perpetrator spent little time with victim after
fatal shooting.

External Injuries:

Single entry wound one inch to the left of sternum. Exit wound
beneath left shoulder blade. Indications that body had been
dragged app. 200 yards to abandoned well. No signs of sexual
molestation. Small abrasion on left side of head from fall to
ground. Interpretation: incident leading to death not impacted
by passion.

Internal Injuries:

None except those created by entering and exiting projectile. No
indications of sexual activity.

Medical Diagnosis:

Cause of death: coronary, caused by perforation of heart by
projectile fired from .22 caliber hand-held weapon approx. 3
feet from victim's chest. Expiration of victim instantaneous.

Notes:

Gruesome. (Word is struck through.)

Time of Death:

Body remained undiscovered for approx. 25 days. Body reveals no external signs of exposure to moisture. Last precipitation in area on October 5. Deduction: body disposed a day following identified rainfall. Decomposition prohibits more accurate time of death.

Investigating Officer: AAD
Recording Officer: JCMc
Typed by: BTM
Date and time: 11/06/2017, 3:05 p.m.
Coroner: Frank R. Holcomb
Received by: Grady C. Calhoun
Further Action: Yes.   Homicide.

Regrets
(A Duologue)

A gun, a pistol, my pistol
is pointed at me and I quake:
What have I done to deserve this.
Have I done anything to deserve this.
What could I have done not to deserve this.
The look in his eyes is one of
"I don't want to do this."

> *I don't want to do this.*
> *But she gives me nothing else to do.*
> *Not do it and we are done.*
> *I can't be done.*
> *Not again.*
> *Not this time.*
> *This is mine.*
> *She is mine.*
> *I claim her as mine.*
> *I will not let her not be mine.*

I regret:
Getting in my car with him for a Sunday afternoon frolic
into the country, away from phones and nosy neighbors,
away from concrete and computers,
away from feelings neither of us understand.
Most recent regret: not saying "No" firmly enough.

> *She said "No"*
> *but did not mean "no."*
> *Who does she think she is,*
> *saying "No."*
> *To me.*
> *No is not acceptable.*
> *No! No "no" allowed!*

I permit "no" no longer.

I regret:
Not asking the girl at the country store
to call for help,
not telling the lady at the pumps
that I am here against my will, taken
into the woods
by a crazed maniac of a man.
Would she have helped?
Was it possible that my cries
would have fallen on inattentive ears?
Never know.
There were no cries.
I am too frightened to cry aloud.

> *Her face says "What!" as*
> *the gun emits its load.*
> *And she crumbles*
> *as if the load is more than she can hold.*
> *What to do?*
> *She has stopped.*
> *Everything. Has stopped.*
> *Can't put her in the car.*
> *Can't leave her here.*
> *Can I? Can I not?*
> *Of course, leave her here.*
> *Where she left me*
> *with nothing else to do.*
> *What do I do now that this is done?*

Regrets:
Leaving Lee, my dear darling Lee.
For what, my freedom?
Fuck freedom, it's not what it's said to be.
Lee, so dear, caring, gentle, easy to read.
Boring, boring Lee.

Foolish me to let him stalk away.
I had no choice.
Probably none.

> *Okay, buried with leaves.*
> *No one will find her*
> *not out here.*
> *not under the leaves.*
> *No one will know she is gone.*
> *Since no one cared.*
> *No one but me.*
> *Isn't that clear?*

Regrets:
Marriage.
Too young.
Too naïve.
Too needy.
Too much romance, not enough truth.
If we had had a child
I would have been clear with it.
Told it the truth about. . . most things.

> *Can't be careless.*
> *Drive with caution.*
> *Leave this place of leaves.*
> *No one will find it.*
> *No one will look.*
> *Could I find it once gone?*
> *Not in this lifetime.*
> *My lifetime, free.*

Regrets:
No children.
No babies.
No diapers.
No sleepless nights.

No children.
Might they have kept us as one?
Two, even, a girl and a boy.
Might things have been different
than this?

> *Ah, this gun,*
> *this thing.*
> *Throw it away.*
> *Can't throw it away.*
> *Expensive.*
> *Bury it with leaves.*
> *Can't bury it.*
> *Important.*
> *It's all that I have.*
> *Don't need it any more,*
> *not now, not after this.*
> *IT IS ALL THAT I HAVE*

Regrets:
Not grading papers.
Not repairing the vacuum.
Not saying "I love you"
when opportunities were ripe.
Not dying of old age.
With Lee.
Is it too late to die of old age?
With Lee?
Will my students forgive me?

> *Momma? Can I come home?*
> *No, Josie's not with me.*
> *We broke up, Josephine and I.*
> *No, can't talk about it.*
> *So, can I? Come home?*
> *Need to get my head straight.*

He has the gun, yes.
But he won't use it.
He can't.
He would regret it.
He regrets.
Never, not here, not yet.
Who is this man?
Do I know him?
Does he have regrets?
Surely, yes.
He, too, can have regrets. . .

A Wake for Josephine

Papa's Lament: Nothing Left

It is not right for a parent, for me,
To outlive his child, my baby.
It is a perversion of the way
Things are intended to be.

I see the coffin, poised to be lowered.
They tell me it holds her body, withered, cold.
The lid is closed, so I am left with nothing and
Believe what I am told.

A dad whose only spawn
Is hidden from his view,
Has little worth remaining
And even less to do.

That is who I am,
The one with no value,
Nothing left but the belief
That the promise of heaven is true.

A better place, that is what they claim,
My baby has gone from here
And resides with angels and harps
And an envious freedom from care.

They tell me this monster
Who put a pistol to my baby's breast
And discharged it without a flinch
Will pay for his crime. That's my request.

I hope his payment is sublime,
That he forfeits the rest of his life,
Locked in a windowless cell,
With cockroaches and rats for spite.

I am asked: Will you forgive this man
If he is found guilty of this deed?
And I say: Yeah, sure, I forgive him,
And may God forgive me my unbearable grief.

I forgive. But I lie, I lie, I lie, I lie! I
Could put a pistol between his eyes
And discharge its load and blow
His brain to darkest hell. With ease.

But if I should, accomplish
Such a vengeful aim,
Who would forgive me?
Or would I be the one all would blame?

I am left alone in this empty shell.
Alone in my newly discovered living hell.

Who among you can understand
That a parent who lives beyond his spawn
Is a parent with nothing left
But an empty, airless, pitiful yawn.

Waiting for Golfers

Characters:
    BLAYNE: A golfer, 28 years old.
    SHERWOOD: A golfer, 28 years old.

Setting: The tee-box on a golf course: a golf cart and two sets of clubs.

(*BLAYNE and SHERWOOD sit in their golf cart, waiting for the groups ahead of them.*)

BLAYNE:
Twenty minutes?

SHERWOOD:
That's what the starter said. Ten, if we're lucky.

BLAYNE:
(*Checking his watch*)
Twenty minutes.

SHERWOOD:
I've waited longer.

BLAYNE:
That foursome ahead of us is gonna make us wait all day. Two couples. Can you believe that?

SHERWOOD:
You want to leave?

BLAYNE:
Of course not. But couples. On a golf course? You've gotta be kidding.
(*He yells forward.*)

It's called golf! G.O.L.F. Gentlemen Only, Ladies
    Forbidden!

SHERWOOD:

Don't do that. They're looking at us.

BLAYNE:

Two places for women: kitchens and bedrooms. In that
    order.
    (Pause)
You have a good week?

SHERWOOD:

More or less. Can't get used to Cheryl being gone. So
    quiet.

BLAYNE:

How long since she - uh—you know—been gone?

SHERWOOD:

Not that she made any unnecessary noise. Miss her for
    her presence. You know? Just being there.

BLAYNE:

You should of just offed her. Taken care of old business.
    Show her who's the man. Not let her walk away like
    she's in charge.

SHERWOOD:

Offed?

(BLAYNE shrugs.)

SHERWOOD:

She wan't too bad. Miss her is all.
    (Pause.)
You?

BLAYNE:

Me what?

SHERWOOD:

How's your week?

BLAYNE:

Bettern yourn, obviously. I know how to take care of my
female problems.

SHERWOOD:

Yeah, you and your right hand

BLAYNE:

In a manner of speaking, you got that right. Just me and
this little old right hand. Comes in handy, knowing
what you gotta do and how you're gonna do it.

SHERWOOD:

(Referring to the golfers ahead of them, big gesture.)
Did you see that? Slice from hell. She'll be looking for
that ball from now 'til sunset. We're gonna be longer
than any ten minutes.

BLAYNE:

Got a decent body on her. Sweet swing. She's had
lessons. Sheez, hitting another ball. Can't they see us
back here, waiting?

SHERWOOD:

(After a pause.)
Think I got my duck hook fixed. Went to Dick's
Sporting Goods and had them video tape me. You
wouldn't believe what I was doing with my left
shoulder.

BLAYNE:

Yeah, I believe it. I been watching that left shoulder
hiccup for the past four years.

SHERWOOD:

And you didn't say anything?

BLAYNE:

What do you take me for—a golf pro? I like winning.

SHERWOOD:

So, I have to drop seventy-five bucks at Dick's because
you relish beating me. Thanks. I'm kicking your ass
today.

BLAYNE:

You and who else?
(Again referring to the golfers ahead of them.)
Did you see that. Twenty yards and he's hitting a second
ball. Didn't get past the women's tee.
(Yelling with an obnoxious voice.)
Texas Rules here, Buddy. He probably don't know what
I'm talking about. We should of gone to Municipal.

SHERWOOD:

Wish you'd stop yelling. They're gonna come back here
and sand wedge us to death.

BLAYNE:

I hate the greens at Municipal. Nothing but target golf,
Municipal. *(Big groan.)* Jeez, another slice into the
deep rough. Can you believe this? Four of them, two
of us, and we're waiting? Should let us play through
and save all of us time and anxiety.

SHERWOOD:

I've played with the guy in the orange shirt before. Pretty
 good putter.
 (Pause.)
Jack said he saw you on the range the other day.

BLAYNE:

What was Jack doing at the driving range?

SHERWOOD:

Target range. Shooting range. You were trying out a new
 pistol, he said.

BLAYNE:

New to me. I got it second hand.

SHERWOOD:

Where from?

BLAYNE:

The getting place.

SHERWOOD:

Got to get me a hand gun one of these days. Shoot me
 some skunks.

BLAYNE:

And ex-wives?

SHERWOOD:

Them, too, maybe. She's got it coming.
 (Pause.)
I'm joking, of course.

BLAYNE:

Then, you should give it to her. Right between the tits.
 Bingo.

SHERWOOD:

Jack said you're pretty good.

BLAYNE:

Jack don't know squat.

SHERWOOD:

Said you had four out of six in the money. Four out of six. That'd make you a sharpshooter.

BLAYNE:

Bond. James Bond.
    (Pause.)
You wanna see it?

SHERWOOD:

What? The target? You brought the target with you to the golf course?

BLAYNE:

My gun.

SHERWOOD:
    (Wait for it.)
Sure.

(BLAYNE takes the pistol from his golf bag.)

BLAYNE:

Try that baby out.

SHERWOOD:

You keep this in your golf bag?

BLAYNE:

Wherever I go, she goes. She makes a bulge when I tote
her in my belt. Golf bag's as good a place as any.
Always handy.

SHERWOOD:
(Taking the gun.)

Whoa, man.

*(SHERWOOD points the pistol in BLAYNE's
direction.)*

BLAYNE:

Careful there, Woody.

SHERWOOD:

Why? It ain't loaded, is it?

BLAYNE:

Now what good is an empty weapon. It's the load that
gives her value.

*(SHERWOOD begins taking the bullets out of the
gun.)*

BLAYNE:

Here. Here, now, what do you think you're doing?

SHERWOOD:

What does it look like?

BLAYNE:

Will you leave my gun alone? Gimme that.
(BLAYNE takes the gun back.)

SHERWOOD:

Hey, you don't have to be . . .

BLAYNE:

Never know when you might need to shoot somebody.
   The guy in the orange shirt, maybe.

SHERWOOD:

Put it away, okay?

BLAYNE:

Or, if you happen to beat me today—

SHERWOOD:

That ain't funny.

BLAYNE:

Well, then. What about Cheryl? She done you dirt.

SHERWOOD:

That's not funny either.

BLAYNE:

Best way to handle a woman. Show her who's boss. I
   may not be boss around many folks these days, but
   this little baby sure is.

SHERWOOD:

Just . . . put it away, okay, Blayne?

BLAYNE:

Makes you uncomfortable, huh?

SHERWOOD:

Somebody might see it.

BLAYNE:
(Pointing the gun at SHERWOOD.)
Do you, Woody? Do you see it?

SHERWOOD:

Hey, man.
> *(Laughs uneasily.)*

Point it someplace else, okay?

BLAYNE:

Wow. There it was again. Just now. The exact same
look. Who would have thunk it.

SHERWOOD:

Maybe we can use it to get this foursome ahead of us to
let us play through.
> *(Laughs. BLAYNE doesn't.)*

Okay. Take the bullets out, okay?

BLAYNE:

I would never have imagined it.

SHERWOOD:

What? What are you talking about?

BLAYNE:

The look. The look in your eyes just then. You couldn't
help it, I know. Same as her. She couldn't help it,
either. Amazing.

SHERWOOD:

Who?

BLAYNE:

Tapper.

SHERWOOD:

Josephine Tapper? You still seeing old cheerleader
Joey?

BLAYNE:

Not any more, no.

SHERWOOD:

I thought she gave you your exit papers three months
  ago. How's she doing?

BLAYNE:
(A nod toward the group ahead of them.)
Okay, we're on deck. Just as soon as these bozos and
  bimbos reach the green, it's game on.

SHERWOOD:

I ain't seen pretty little Joey in a long time. Is she okay?

BLAYNE:

Not likely to see her again, either. She's long gone.

SHERWOOD:

Left town?

BLAYNE:

In a manner of speaking. Yeah, left.

SHERWOOD:
(After a beat.)
What look?

BLAYNE:

Huh?

SHERWOOD:

A minute ago, you said I gave you the same look as
  something or other. What were you talking about?

BLAYNE:

It was the same look I saw in Tapper's eyes just before.

SHERWOOD:

Before what?

BLAYNE:

It was a look of disbelief. Fear. Mixed with regret. Maybe a little bit of doubt. Then horror. Then hate.

SHERWOOD:

Before what.

BLAYNE:

I mean. . . I'm no damn philosopher, you know. Not much for making sense out of things. But that moment, that very special, unforgettable moment when the thought entered her female pea-sized brain that maybe, just maybe it was me who was in control, that maybe I not only had this but I also had the cause. And there, right then, with nobody around, just her and me, out in the middle of nowhere, I had the opportunity. What is it they say on those TV cop shows? Means, motive, and opportunity? I had all three. And I also had that look of—I don't know what to call it. Terror? Mortality? The invitation to depart this moral coil?

SHERWOOD:

Mortal.

BLAYNE:

Hm?

SHERWOOD:

This Mortal Coil. It's Shakespeare.

BLAYNE:

Whatever, man. Tapper and me, the last time we were
together that way, went to her great uncle's funeral. I
didn't care much for dear old Great Uncle Ted. I
don't care much for church, especially funerals, but
she insisted. And the preacher gets up there and has
the gall to proclaim that poor Uncle Ted—suffered
for eight months from excruciating pain—lung
cancer—had been give a gift—the gift of life in a better
place. The man seemed to actually believe what he
was saying: "Going to a Better Place." "The Happy
Hunting Ground." Something like that. Tapper and
me had this big blow-out on the way home after her
Uncle had been lowered into the earth. She felt that
I was being sacrilegious or something—not believing.
I mean, Woody, think about it. If death is the
gateway to something better, then why the hell is
suicide illegal? If I believed such a thing as that, I'd
be hopping in front of every freight train I see. And
taking everybody I loved with me. You, maybe.
   (Pause.)
Tell me, man, just then. When I pointed a loaded gun at
you. What did you think?
   (SHERWOOD turns away.)
No, don't back off. Tell me. What did you think? What
went through your head?

SHERWOOD:

I wasn't thinking about the Happy Hunting Ground.

BLAYNE:

Should hope not. Were you afraid I would pull the
trigger?

SHERWOOD:

Ah, knock it off, Blayne. We're up.

BLAYNE:

This moral coil. No, what did you call it? Mortal? This
mortal coil? The look in her eyes. The knowledge
that her mortal coil was about to spring apart. She
didn't believe that I'd pull the trigger either. She was
convinced that she was destined to live out her life
on this hell of an earth. That she wouldn't have to go
to some place better, not until she had suffered
enough pain and agony to make dying worthwhile.
But the look she had. Stupid. Isn't it true: if you
believe something, you believe it completely, without
reservation? Why, then, that look of complete terror
on her face? If she was right—and by God, she
almost had me convinced—she's some place better
right now, looking on all of this and saying: Pull it
again, Blayne pull the coil apart again. Just for the
fun of it, Sherwood, do you believe the same as
Tapper, that we live in order to gain access to a
better life someplace else? Huh? Do you?
   (Pause.)
Ah, fuck it.
   *(He returns the gun to his golf bag and takes out his
   driver.)*
Let's play golf.

   *(BLAYNE approaches the tee box. After a lengthy
   pause.)*

SHERWOOD:

Did you, Blayne? Did you kill Josephine Tapper?

BLAYNE:

Jesus. What do you take me for, Sherwood? Ha!

*(BLAYNE laughs lightly as he practices his golf swing.
   SHERWOOD stares at BLAYNE's golf bag where*

the pistol is stowed. He looks back at his golfing partner as the lights fade.

Black out.

End.)

A Killer's Hands

I got no poetry.
Poems and me don't mix.
What I got
is what I know
and if I know it,
it must be true.

Cops got no poetry either.
If they had poetry,
they wouldn't have
put us in the same cell.
Us—that's me
and that killer,
name of Blayne.

Same cell, two nights.
Two nights in a cell
is a lifetime for some.
"What they got you for?"
I ask, being neighborly.
And he says right out,
"I killed my girl."

That's how he said it
like he was glad to
be shed of it.
Know I would be,
glad and all.
"I killed my girl."
Nothing else.

Not even after I asked
him straight up—
"How come?"
And he said nothing.
Just sat there on his cell bunk
staring at his hands.
His killer hands.

Justice

After a nine-day jury trial,
Crumbley is found guilty
as charged of
second degree murder.
He is sentenced to serve
a term of life imprisonment
at hard labor
without benefit of probation,
parole, or suspension of sentence.

Justice is done:

"I believe that with all my heart,"
the father says.

A Wake for Josephine

Alone

I confess.
I did not do
what you all say I did.
She did it herself,
pointed the gun and
pulled the trigger.
On herself.

Her last words.
Blayne, I . . .
Last words.
Her last.
Blayne, I . . .
My name.
On her lips.
Just that.
Nothing else.
Just my name.
And she did it.
Did herself in.
One pop.
Little pop.
Pop like a cap.
Pop and done.

Then she fell.
I could tell when she fell,
she was gone.
And I screamed—
No!
She didn't hear.
Couldn't hear.
Stop!
She couldn't.
She was gone.

Like a puff of smoke.
Or a twig under foot.
Gone like that.
Pop.

Christ! I yelled.
He didn't hear.
He wasn't there.
Not in those woods.
Not there then.
Not there now.
Not there ever.

What I did then
I cannot tell.
I don't recall.

Too much alone.

Then and now.

So much alone.

About the Author

Kenneth Robbins grew up on a chicken farm in Northwest Georgia, the son of James Aubrey and Inez Graham Robbins, and was educated in a three-room schoolhouse in Bill Arp, Georgia, until he finished the seventh grade. At the age of twelve, he discovered Jack Schaefer's novella, *Shane,* and fell in love with the joy that reading provided. He published his first short story at the age of seventeen in the Beta Club Journal for which he received $5.00, and he was hooked for life.

His first novel, *Buttermilk Bottoms,* received the Associated Writing Programs Novel Award and was published by the University of Iowa Press. It was also presented the Toni Morrison Prize for Fiction, one of the McDonald's Literary Awards. His most recent publication is his short story collection, *Christmas Brittle* (Adelaide Books) and *Atomic Field* by NewStage Press, forthcoming.

He holds degrees from Young Harris College (Associate of Arts), Georgia Southern University (Bachelor of Science), the University of Georgia (Master of Fine Arts in Theatre), and Southern Illinois University (Doctor of Philosophy in Speech). He retired from full-time teaching after a 48-year career that included stints as the Director of the School of the Performing Arts, Louisiana Tech University, and Chair of the Department of Speech and Theatre, Newberry College, Newberry, South Carolina. He lives with his wife, Dorothy Dodge Robbins, the Charlotte Lewis Endowed Professor of English,

Louisiana Tech, with whom he has co-edited 4 collections of literary works, including *Christmas Stories from Louisiana* (UP Mississippi).

Kenneth is by trade a playwright having written over 100 scripts for the stage with most receiving world premieres. Among his more ambitious works are *Matchless*, recipient of the Festival of Southern Theatre Award, *Atomic Field,* winner of the Charles Getchell New Play Award, presented through the Southeastern Theatre Conference, and *The Dallas File,* winner of the Florida Theatre Conference New Play Award. His radio play, "Dynamite Hill," was produced by the National Radio Theatre, starring Brock Peters, as the pilot for a proposed series of dramas dealing with the Black experience in America. The production received a Corporation for Public Broadcasting Program Award, a Gabriel Society Humanitarian Award, and the text was selected for airing by BBC Radio 3. His works for the stage have been produced throughout the United States, Canada, Ireland, England, Denmark, and Japan.

As an academic, Dr. Robbins is a past recipient of a Fulbright Award to teach American literature and culture in Skopje, North Macedonia. He received a Malone Fellowship to participate in a two-week study excursion in Saudi Arabia, a Japan Foundation Artists Fellowship to research and live in Japan, a Hawthornden Castle Fellowship to write for a month in Scotland, and a Fundacion Valparaiso Fellowship to work for a month in Southern Spain. He served as a judge, the Cairo International Festival of Experimental Theatre, a lecturer in Tel Aviv, Israel, and guest speaker on the topic, "On Being an Hibakusha" in Tokyo, Japan.

Currently, he is working on a new novel about coming of age during the atomic era, a collection of one-act plays dealing with Will Shakespeare as a husband, and teaching within the Honors Program at Louisiana Tech University.

Additional Works

Buttermilk Bottoms, a Novel, recipient of the Toni Morrison Prize and the Associated Writing Programs Novel Award

The City of Churches, a Novel

At Sea on the Nile, a Novel

Matchless or How Savannah Was Spared the Torch, a Novel

Atomic Field, recipient of the Charles Getchell New Play Award

Molly's Rock, recipient of the Western Illinois University New Play Award

The Dallas File, recipient of the Florida Theatre Conference New Play Award

The One Stop Café, recipient of the Festival of Southern Theatre Award

Iron Mountain, a Novel

Christmas Brittle, Seasonal Fictions, collection of short fiction

www.ingramcontent.com/pod-product-compliance
Lightning Source LLC
Chambersburg PA
CBHW071827020426
42331CB00007B/1636